NATIONAL
GEOGRAPHIC

T0045495

Weather Today

Marvin Buckley

I know what the weather
will be like today.
I looked out my bedroom window.

It's going to be sunny today.
That's why I am wearing my hat.
It will protect my face from the sun.

I know what the weather
will be like today.
I stepped outside to see
how warm it is.

It's going to be cool today.
That's why I am wearing my sweater.
It will help to keep me warm.

I know what the weather
will be like today.
I asked my mom.

It's going to be rainy today.
That's why I am wearing my raincoat.
It will help to keep me dry.

I know what the weather
will be like today.
I watched the weather report
on television.
It's going to be nice today.